W9-BDK-977

NEWBURYPORT PUBLIC LIBRARY
94 STATE STREET
NEWBURYPORT, MA 01950

IN THE ZONE

CHEERLEADING

DON WELLS

MEDIA ENHANCED BOOKS
AV²
BY WEIGL
ADDED VALUE · AUDIO VISUAL

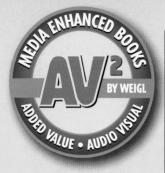

BOOK CODE

K108963

AV² **by Weigl** brings you media enhanced books that support active learning.

AV² provides enriched content that supplements and complements this book. Weigl's AV² books strive to create inspired learning and engage young minds for a total learning experience.

Go to **www.av2books.com**, and enter this book's unique code. You will have access to video, audio, web links, quizzes, a slide show, and activities.

Audio
Listen to sections of the book read aloud.

Video
Watch informative video clips.

Web Link
Find research sites and play interactive games.

Try This!
Complete activities and hands-on experiments.

Due to the dynamic nature of the Internet, some of the URLs and activities provided as part of AV² by Weigl may have changed or ceased to exist. AV² by Weigl accepts no responsibility for any such changes. All media enhanced books are regularly monitored to update addresses and sites in a timely manner. Contact AV² by Weigl at 1-866-649-3445 or av2books@weigl.com with any questions, comments, or feedback.

Published by AV² by Weigl
350 5th Avenue, 59th Floor
New York, NY 10118
Website: www.av2books.com   www.weigl.com

Copyright © 2011 AV² by Weigl
All rights reserved. No part of this publication may be reproduced, stored in a retrieval system, or transmitted in any form or by any means, electronic, mechanical, photocopying, recording, or otherwise, without the prior written permission of Weigl Publishers Inc.

Library of Congress Cataloging-in-Publication Data available upon request.
Fax 1-866-44-WEIGL for the attention of the Publishing Records department.

ISBN 978-1-60596-895-7 (hard cover)
ISBN 978-1-60596-896-4 (soft cover)

Printed in the United States in North Mankato, Minnesota
1 2 3 4 5 6 7 8 9   14 13 12 11 10

052010
WEP264000

PROJECT COORDINATOR Heather C. Hudak   **DESIGN** Terry Paulhus

Every reasonable effort has been made to trace ownership and to obtain permission to reprint copyright material. The publishers would be pleased to have any errors or omissions brought to their attention so that they may be corrected in subsequent printings.

Weigl acknowledges Getty Images as its primary image supplier for this title.

CONTENTS

For centuries, **spectators** have cheered for people playing sports. Still, cheerleading did not **officially** begin until 1898. Johnny Campbell, a student at the University of Minnesota, led the crowd at a football game in a famous cheer. He yelled, "Rah, Rah, Rah! Sku-u-mar, Hoo-Rah! Hoo-Rah! Varsity! Varsity! Varsity, Minn-e-So-Tah!" This cheer is still used. Those who use it today use the name of their team or school.

By the 1950s, cheerleading had become common in American high schools. Most cheerleaders at this time were girls.

Cheerleading is more than leading crowds in cheers. Cheerleaders perform **routines** to entertain spectators. They urge players on sports teams to do well. The first American cheerleading **squads** performed at colleges in the eastern part of the United States during the 1800s. Squad members were all men.

During the 1970s, cheerleading became a very popular sport. Squads focused on strength and stunts. They **competed** with other cheerleading squads.

Today, cheerleading is one of the fastest growing sports. Cheerleading squads in 43 countries participate in competitions. Nearly 4 million people participate in cheerleading in the United States.

A cheerleader's uniform should be light so he or she can jump, dance, and move quickly. Cheerleaders do not need much equipment to perform their routines.

Women often wear short skirts with matching bloomers, or briefs, underneath. Bloomers are also called "spankies" and "lollies."

Pompoms come in a variety of bright colors. Usually, they are the team's colors. Pompoms help the crowd see cheerleaders' hand and arm movements.

Cheerleaders wear comfortable shoes such as running shoes or cross-trainers.

Many cheerleaders use pompoms. The first pompoms were made of crepe paper. Around 1965, Fred Gastoff invented vinyl pompoms. **Metallic** red, gold, and blue are the most common pompom colors.

■ Megaphones magnify a cheerleader's voice so that cheers are easier to hear in a large crowd.

The megaphone can also be an important part of a cheerleader's equipment. A megaphone is a cone-shaped device held to the mouth to boost and direct the voice. Cheerleaders have used megaphones since 1898 to help crowds hear their cheers.

■ Cheerleaders use props, such as flags, to help excite the crowd.

Performing

Cheerleaders perform their routines at sporting events such as football or basketball games. They lead the crowd in cheers from the sidelines of the playing field or gymnasium. During breaks in the game, cheerleaders perform longer routines. Their performances keep the crowd excited about the game.

Cheerleaders perform at **pep rallies** and other school events to promote school spirit. Routines can be performed in school auditoriums, lunchrooms, gymnasiums, or sports stadiums.

■ Cheerleaders amaze crowds at sporting events with their skills and stunts.

Cheerleading competitions usually take place on a stage. Squads that compete perform **tumbles** and other complicated movements on mats. Mats help prevent injuries.

During a performance, a cheerleading squad will sometimes perform many different stunts at once.

Cheerleading Basics

There are two types of cheerleaders: spirit squads and competitive teams. Spirit squads cheer for sports teams and perform at sporting events. Competitive teams, also called drill teams, usually perform at competitions. Some competitive teams also perform at sporting events.

Spirit squads use chants and cheers to keep the crowd interested in the game and encourage their team. Spirit squads use tumbling, lifts, tosses, and dance moves set to music to entertain the crowd.

■ Cheerleaders display impressive balance and strength in their moves.

■ Cheers or chants are often done to specific dance moves.

Competitive teams develop and perform **synchronized** two-minute or three-minute routines. Coaches often **choreograph** and help squads rehearse the routines. Competitive teams also use tumbling, lifts, tosses, and dance moves set to music.

In some routines, strong cheerleaders, called bases, lift smaller cheerleaders, called flyers. Flyers are sometimes thrown high into the air and caught before they hit the ground. Cheerleading squads also build human pyramids. During competitions, teams receive scores for their routines from judges. The winner is the squad with the highest score.

Cheerleaders often perform dangerous moves and stunts. They do not wear **protective** gear. To help prevent injuries, the National Federation of State High Schools Association created safety rules for all American school-based cheerleading squads. These rules cover all **techniques** cheerleaders use.

Cheerleaders must learn to trust their teammates. All members rely on each other for safety.

11

heerleaders must have coordination and a good sense of timing. They must be able to perform tumbling and dance moves as well.

Cheerleaders perform **precise** movements. All members of a squad often make the same motions at the same time. Cheerleaders add small changes to basic motions to make the movements more entertaining. Cheerleaders also use **gymnastic** moves with many jumps in their routines.

Cheerleading routines often include the splits.

Cheerleading routines often involve stunts performed by two or more cheerleaders. Specially trained coaches teach stunts. Cheerleaders use **spotters** who can catch them if they fall while attempting a stunt.

One stunt is called the cradle. Several cheerleaders act as bases. They throw a flyer, who is standing on the bases' hands, into the air. The flyer rises into the air and lands back in the bases' arms. Another stunt is the elevator. The bases push a flyer up until the bases' arms are straight above their heads.

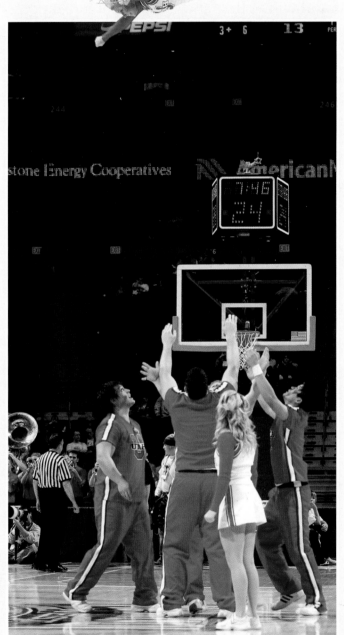

Many cheerleading squads blend dance moves, music, and acrobatics in their routines.

Flyers must time their acrobatic moves perfectly so the bases can catch them safely.

Cheerleading Groups

The United States has many cheerleading **organizations**. Most of these groups try to make cheerleading a safe sport.

In 1948, Laurence "Hurkie" Hurkimer founded the first cheerleading organization, the National Cheerleading Association (NCA). He organized the first cheerleader camp at Sam Houston University in Huntsville, Texas. Fifty-two girls attended the camp. Within a few years, 20,000 girls were attending Hurkimer's camps.

The NCA now sponsors championships for all levels of cheerleading squads. The most important event hosted by the NCA is the Chick-fil-A Cheer and Dance Collegiate Championship. More than 140 university cheerleading squads from the United States, Canada, Japan, and Mexico compete in this competition. It is shown on network television.

Many cheerleaders attend camps and workshops to perfect stunts, such as rolls and flips.

Cheerleading camps are a great place to meet new people.

A cheerleader from the University of Kansas, Randy L. Neil, established the International Cheerleading Foundation (ICF) in 1964. The ICF hosted the first nationally televised cheerleading competition in 1978.

The ICF became the World Cheerleading Association (WCA) in 1995. The WCA has members in the United States, England, Germany, Ireland, and Scotland. More than 5,000 cheerleading squads have competed at the WCA Nationals.

Jeff Webb, a cheerleader at the University of Oklahoma, founded the Universal Cheerleaders Association (UCA) in 1974. The UCA started the National High School Cheerleading Championships in 1979.

Though there are many cheerleading competitions nationwide, the National Collegiate Athletic Association does not recognize the sport.

More than 220 U.S. colleges, including the University of Florida, offer cheerleading scholarships.

Professional Cheerleading

The first professional sports team to have cheerleaders was the National Football League's (NFL) Baltimore Colts. The Colts introduced cheerleaders in 1960. In 1984, the Colts moved to Indianapolis. Cheerleading is still an important part of every Colts game.

The Washington Redskins cheerleaders are the oldest active cheerleading squad in the NFL. The squad, called the Redskinettes, was formed in 1962. Besides cheering for the Redskins, the cheerleaders have raised millions of dollars for charity. They have toured China to promote U.S.-made products. They have even entertained U.S. military troops serving in foreign countries.

The Washington Redskins cheerleaders are also known as the "First Ladies of Football."

While games are in play, professional cheerleaders entertain from the sidelines.

In 1972, the Dallas Cowboys cheerleaders added Broadway-style jazz dancing to their cheerleading routines. When the Dallas Cowboys cheerleaders appeared on television at Super Bowl X in 1976, the public became more aware of professional cheerleaders. After this event, most NFL teams created cheerleading squads. Each NFL cheerleading team has 30 members.

■ The average career for a professional cheerleader lasts five years.

Basketball cheerleaders are often called dancers. Unlike the NFL, the number of cheerleaders on basketball cheerleading teams varies. Many professional cheerleading squads also offer junior teams.

■ Tryouts for professional cheerleading teams are very competitive. Hundreds try out for very few positions.

Cheerleading Superstars

Cheerleaders entertain fans and amaze crowds with their tumbling and dance moves. Many famous people have been cheerleaders.

Miley Cyrus

BIRTH DATE: November 23, 1992
HOMETOWN: Franklin, Tennessee

CAREER FACTS:
- Cyrus is a well-known actress and singer who stars in the television show *Hannah Montana*.
- Cyrus was a cheerleader at Heritage Middle School in Tennessee.

Carrie Underwood

BIRTH DATE: March 10, 1983
HOMETOWN: Checotah, Oklahoma

CAREER FACTS:
- Since winning *American Idol*, Underwood has sold more than 10 million albums and has won four Grammy awards.
- Underwood was a cheerleader at Checotah High School in Oklahoma.

Halle Berry

BIRTH DATE: August 14, 1968
HOMETOWN: Cleveland, Ohio

CAREER FACTS:
- Berry is an Oscar-winning actress who has starred in films such as *X-Men* and *Catwoman*.
- Berry was a cheerleader at Bedford High School in Cleveland.

Samuel L. Jackson

BIRTH DATE: December 21, 1948
HOMETOWN: Washington, D.C.

CAREER FACTS:
- Jackson has starred in many films, including *The Incredibles*, *Star Wars Episode I*, and *Unbreakable*. He has acted in more than 100 movies and television shows.
- Jackson was a cheerleader at his high school in Chattanooga, Tennessee.

George W. Bush

BIRTH DATE: July 6, 1946
HOMETOWN: New Haven, Connecticut

CAREER FACTS:
- Bush served as the 43rd president of the United States.
- Bush was head cheerleader when he attended the all-boys Phillips Academy in Andover, Massachusetts.

Staying Healthy

Cheerleading requires jumping, tumbling, and other types of **energetic** movements. A healthy diet is important for cheerleaders.

Eating carbohydrates, such as bread, pasta, whole grains, vegetables, and fruits, provides cheerleaders with energy. Protein from meat and eggs builds muscles. Calcium in dairy products also keeps bones strong.

Drinking plenty of water before, during, and after cheerleading routines is important. Water helps keep people's bodies cool. When cheerleaders sweat, they lose water. Drinking water replaces what is lost through sweat during a routine. Cheerleaders should avoid sugary drinks.

Eating a wide variety of healthy foods, including whole-grain bread, fruits, vegetables, and milk products, is an important part of any diet.

Cheerleaders need strong, flexible muscles. Stretching keeps muscles flexible. It is best to stretch after a **warmup**. Running in place or jogging warms muscles and helps prevent injuries.

It is easy to twist an ankle while performing cheerleading routines. Wearing heel inserts in shoes can help reduce the risk of foot and ankle injuries. Wearing cross-trainers with good support helps, too.

To hold poses and perform stunts, cheerleaders need strong muscles.

Test your knowledge of this exciting sport by trying to answer these cheerleading brain teasers!

1 Where do cheerleaders perform their routines?

2 When did cheerleading officially start?

3 Name two pieces of equipment used by cheerleaders.

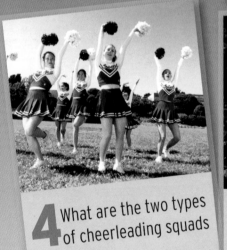

4 What are the two types of cheerleading squads or teams?

5 What types of skills do cheerleaders need to join a cheerleading squad?

6 Which cheerleading squad is the oldest active squad in the NFL?

ANSWERS: 1. Cheerleaders perform their routines at sporting events such as football or basketball games. They also perform at pep rallies and other school events. 2. Cheerleading officially started in 1898 at the University of Minnesota. 3. Cheerleaders often use pompoms and megaphones. 4. The two types of cheerleading squads are spirit squads and competitive teams. 5. Cheerleaders must have coordination and a good sense of timing. They must be able to perform tumbling and dance moves as well. 6. The Washington Redskins cheerleaders are the oldest active cheerleading squad in the NFL.

Glossary

choreograph: plan cheerleading or dance routines

competed: tried to win

energetic: requiring a large amount of energy

gymnastic: acrobatic moves that require strength and balance

metallic: shiny, looks like metal

officially: formally

organizations: groups of people who work together

pep rallies: events to encourage school spirit

precise: exact

protective: to cover or shield from injury

routines: series of steps or moves

spectators: people who watch something without taking part

spotters: people who watch someone performing a stunt and offer assistance if required

squads: small groups of cheerleaders who perform routines together

synchronized: perform the same movements at the same time

techniques: specific ways to perform moves in a sport

tumbles: feats such as somersaults, cartwheels, and handsprings

warmup: gentle exercise to get a person's body ready for stretching and game play

Index

Log on to www.av2books.com

AV² by Weigl brings you media enhanced books that support active learning. Go to **www.av2books.com**, and enter the special code inside the front cover of this book. You will gain access to enriched and enhanced content that supplements and complements this book. Content includes video, audio, web links, quizzes, a slide show, and activities.

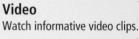

Audio
Listen to sections of the book read aloud.

Video
Watch informative video clips.

Web Link
Find research sites and play interactive games.

Try This!
Complete activities and hands-on experiments.

WHAT'S ONLINE?

Try This! Complete activities and hands-on experiments.	Web Link Find research sites and play interactive games.	Video Watch informative video clips.	**EXTRA FEATURES**
Pages 6-7 Test your knowledge of cheerleading equipment.	**Pages 4-5** Find out more information about the history of cheerleading.	**Pages 4-5** Watch a video of cheerleaders in action.	**Audio** Hear introductory audio at the top of every page
Pages 8-9 Try writing your own cheerleading chant.	**Pages 8-9** Learn how to create a cheerleading chant.	**Pages 18-19** View an interview with a cheerleader.	**Key Words** Study vocabulary, and play a matching word game.
Pages 12-13 Test your knowledge of moves and stunts.	**Pages 10-11** Learn more about cheerleading basics.		
Pages 16-17 Write a biography about one of the superstars of cheerleading.	**Pages 12-13** Read about different types of cheerleading moves.		**Slide Show** View images and captions, and try a writing activity.
Pages 20-21 Play an interactive game.	**Pages 14-15** Learn about cheerleading groups.		**AV² Quiz** Take this quiz to test your knowledge
Page 22 Test your cheerleading knowledge.	**Pages 20-21** Find out more about stretching and exercising.		

Due to the dynamic nature of the Internet, some of the URLs and activities provided as part of AV2 by Weigl may have changed or ceased to exist. AV2 by Weigl accepts no responsibility for any such changes. All media enhanced books are regularly monitored to update addresses and sites in a timely manner. Contact AV2 by Weigl at 1-866-649-3445 or av2books@weigl.com with any questions, comments, or feedback.